I0813138

HISTORICAL AGES

THE FORMATIVE PERIOD

BY SUE BRADFORD EDWARDS

CONTENT CONSULTANT
Christopher Morgan, PhD
Professor, Department of Anthropology
University of Nevada, Reno

Core Library
An Imprint of Abdo Publishing
abdobooks.com

Cover image: During the Formative Period, people began farming crops. This marked the shift from the Archaic to the Formative.

abdobooks.com

Published by Abdo Publishing, a division of ABDO, PO Box 398166, Minneapolis, Minnesota 55439.

Printed in the United States of America, North Mankato, Minnesota.
102024
012025

Cover Photo: North Wind Picture Archives/Alamy
Interior Photos: Kent Raney/Shutterstock Images, 4–5; Carver Mostardi/Alamy, 7; Shutterstock Images, 9, 12, 14–15, 32 (symbols); Zack Frank/Shutterstock Images, 17; Robert Alexander/Archive Photos/Getty Images, 19; Marcl Schauer/Shutterstock Images, 23, 45; DEA Picture Library/De Agostini/Getty Images, 26–27, 43; Peter Hermes Furian/Shutterstock Images, 32 (numerals); Craig Lovell/Corbis Documentary/Getty Images, 33; Christian Vinces/Shutterstock Images, 36–37; Red Line Editorial, 40

Editor: Laura Stickney
Series Designer: Ryan Gale

Library of Congress Control Number: 2024938372

Publisher's Cataloging-in-Publication Data

Names: Edwards, Sue Bradford, author.
Title: The Formative period / by Sue Bradford Edwards
Description: Minneapolis, Minnesota: ABDO Publishing, 2025 | Series: Historical ages | Includes online resources and index.
Identifiers: ISBN 9781098295639 (lib. bdg.) | ISBN 9798384916635 (ebook)
Subjects: LCSH: History, Ancient--Juvenile literature. | Land settlement--Juvenile literature. | Agriculture--Juvenile literature. | Weaving--Juvenile literature. | History--Juvenile literature. | Historical archaeology--Juvenile literature. | Civilization and science--Juvenile literature. | Anthropology, Prehistoric--Juvenile literature.
Classification: DDC 930.11--dc23

CONTENTS

CHAPTER ONE

THE MISSISSIPPIANS

The tour group had climbed 154 steps to the top of Monks Mound in Cahokia, Illinois. Now they followed the guide to the mound's center. The guide said that Monks Mound was about 955 feet (291 m) long and 775 feet (236 m) wide. It was the center of a city during the Formative Period, from 1000 CE to 1400 CE.

The guide said that archaeologists call the people who once lived there Mississippians. This name is based on the Mississippi River

Monks Mound is the largest human-made earthwork in North America. It includes four raised terraces, or levels.

valley, where their culture developed. To build Monks Mound, the Mississippians dug clay and sandy soil with stone hoes and carried the soil to the mound site in woven baskets. Then they dumped the soil, which sometimes remained in the shape of the basket. More soil was carried over and loosely scattered. Other sections were built of sod blocks. Sod is grass, its roots, and soil cut into blocks or strips. The blocks were stacked to build part of Monks Mound. The Mississippian people built this mound over

EFFIGY MOUNDS

During the Late Woodland Period (600–1250 CE), a group known as the Effigy Mound Culture built mounds in what are now the states of Wisconsin, Minnesota, Iowa, and Ohio. The mounds were likely built between 750 CE and 1200 CE. They are shaped like snakes, birds, bears, bison, and panthers. Some archaeologists believe these mounds marked ceremonial centers where people gathered at certain times every year. Others think the mounds marked boundaries. Visitors can see mounds at Effigy Mounds National Monument in Iowa and Serpent Mound Historical Site in Ohio.

Mississippian people at Cahokia used stone hoes for digging and breaking up earth. These tools often had stone blades made of chert, a type of rock. The blades were attached to wooden handles.

100 years, starting sometime from 900 to 950 CE or 1050 CE to 1150 CE. It was the biggest mound in the city.

Someone in the tour group asked where the city was now. The guide said that to understand the ancient people's story, the group needed to understand what drew them to the area. Three rivers—the Mississippi, Missouri, and Illinois—meet in the area. Spring rains cause the rivers to flood, which leaves behind rich soil. Early people lived in and around Cahokia for many years before people began building mounds. People who built mounds at the site gathered plants, fished, and hunted animals. But they also grew squash and sunflowers. The Mississippian people grew more than they could eat. This meant that not everyone had to farm. Cahokia was at its largest in about 1100 CE, when 15,000 to 20,000 people lived there. It was bigger than London, United Kingdom, and Paris, France, were at that time. It was also the largest prehistoric North American city north of Mexico.

The people of Cahokia traded with other peoples. They exchanged items such as salt and chert, a stone used to make tools. They also traded decorated pottery.

The people of Cahokia built about 120 mounds at the site. Buildings such as temples and the leader's home sat on flat-topped mounds, such as Monks Mound. Ridge-topped mounds had rectangular bases and ridged tops. These mounds marked boundaries, while cone-shaped mounds were used for burials.

The guide explained that people in Cahokia built structures with the materials they had on hand. Homes were built of wooden poles. Archaeologists found the

Archaeologists have found remains of five Woodhenge circles at Cahokia, each with a different number of poles. The third circle was reconstructed in 1985.

wall trenches where the poles once stood. The guide pointed out a circle of standing logs in the distance. This was Woodhenge, reconstructed by archaeologists. Woodhenge was an observatory that people may have used as a calendar. It marked the dates when the moon or sun lined up with the tops of the logs. On these dates, people held seasonal festivals. The Mississippians built Woodhenge out of red cedar logs. They used a mineral called ochre to paint the logs red.

FECAL STANOLS

Feces is a scientific word for poop. Fecal stanols are very tiny particles. Digesting meat produces more fecal stanols than digesting plants. Humans produce more fecal stanols than other animals. A. J. White is an archaeologist from the University of California, Berkeley. In 2018, he gathered soil samples from below Horseshoe Lake, which is outside Cahokia. The amount of fecal stanols in the soil suggested that there was a low human population in the area in 1400 CE, and that people started returning to the area in 1500 CE.

Next, the guide pointed out the palisade, a rebuilt portion of the wall of upright logs. The original wall protected the center of the city and had been built by 1150 CE. Around this time, the city's population declined as people moved away.

By 1400 CE, the city had been nearly abandoned. Archaeologists are unsure why. Some believe it was because drought and floods destroyed crops. But in 2018, archaeologists found evidence that people didn't leave the area entirely. Most people moved to other areas where they farmed, planted gardens, and hunted bison. A few people stayed in Cahokia, and eventually people who had moved returned. People who visit this site today can learn about how the Mississippians lived. The Mississippians are part of what is known as the Formative Period.

WHAT IS THE FORMATIVE PERIOD?

The Mississippians thrived during the Formative Period. This period falls between the Archaic and Classic Periods. Because parts of these periods overlap, the Formative is sometimes called the Post-Archaic. Early archaeologists viewed the Formative as a period that all cultures went through as they grew into complex societies. But later, they realized people in different areas didn't follow the same paths of cultural change. This means the Formative looked different in different places.

Before the Formative Period, ancient people lived as hunter-gatherers. They moved from place to place

In archaeology, the term *formative* describes cultures that have developed farming practices and permanent settlements. During the Formative Period, crops became an important food source for people throughout the Americas.

to find food. But during the Formative Period, people grew crops such as maize. Maize is another word for corn. As people grew food, they built villages. People in these villages developed special skills. Some made pottery, while others wove cloth. As people settled, they no longer needed to carry all their belongings.

When archaeologists study Formative cultures, they often focus on Mesoamerica. This region includes

Mexico and Central America. In Mesoamerica, the Early Formative Period began in approximately 1500 BCE, while the Late Formative Period ended in 900 CE. In parts of North America, the Formative Period spanned from around 1000 BCE to 1450 CE. The dates differ because different groups of people settled and began to rely on farming at different times. During the Formative Period, people shaped their environment in important ways. They farmed fields. They built large structures. They developed complex societies.

EXPLORE ONLINE

Chapter One discusses the Mississippian settlement at Cahokia. The website below gives more information about the settlement. As you know, every source is different. How is the information from the website the same as the information in Chapter One? What new information did you learn from the website?

EXPLORE CAHOKIA MOUNDS

abdocorelibrary.com/formative-period

CHAPTER TWO

NORTH AMERICA

During the Formative Period, several cultures developed in North America. In the Early Formative, people settled in villages to grow crops such as maize. Maize was bred from teosinte, a wild Mexican grass. When people traveled, they shared knowledge of how to grow maize. The practice of farming spread.

One Early Formative culture was the Ancestral Puebloan, which arose in what is now the southwestern United States from

At the Canyons of the Ancients Visitor Center and Museum in Colorado, people can see a replica of an early Ancestral Puebloan pit house.

about 500 CE to 1300 CE. Pueblo I is a subperiod of the Early Formative in this region. It spanned from 750 CE to 900 CE. Before the Early Formative, Ancestral Puebloans lived in pit dwellings, or round homes dug into the ground. During the Early Formative, people built aboveground homes made of wattle and daub.

Settlements soon took the form of pueblos. Pueblos are multifamily homes with multiple rooms. The largest pueblos were villages with more than 100 rooms. Most were likely occupied for only 10 to 40 years. Each family lived in a large room. They stored food in small side rooms. Although people still collected wild foods, their main food was maize. Farming this crop was a way to gather extra food in the desert region.

WOODLAND CULTURE

The Woodland is another Early Formative North American culture. Woodland peoples were known for building mounds. Archaeologists think ancient peoples in the eastern United States began building mounds in

Three of the original 18 mounds remain at Plum Bayou Mounds Archeological State Park. The site is a National Historic Landmark.

about 3500 BCE. One Early Formative site is Crowley's Ridge in Helena, Arkansas. It includes five burial mounds. Two of the mounds, which date from 100 BCE to 100 CE, were excavated in 1960. Archaeologists discovered 28 burials in them. The graves contained trade goods that belonged to wealthy or powerful people. These included copper items, shell beads, conch shells, and a mineral called mica.

Another Early Formative site, the Plum Bayou Mounds, is located southeast of Little Rock, Arkansas.

It dates from 650 CE to 1050 CE. Archaeologists discovered food remains at the site. This included two North American grasses, little barley and maygrass. Other food remains discovered at Plum Bayou were a wild vegetable called lamb's-quarter and a grain called amaranth.

Archaeologists have found evidence of maize in the eastern United States dating from at least 200 CE. Archaeologists can tell whether ancient people ate maize in two ways. Sometimes they find burnt corn that fell into a fire during cooking. Other times, they use a process called stable-isotope analysis, which can reveal chemicals from corn in the bones and teeth of skeletons. Woodland peoples had begun to settle before they learned to grow corn.

PUEBLO II

For Ancestral Puebloans, the Middle Formative Period is called Pueblo II. It occurred in the southwestern United States between 900 CE and 1150 CE. During this

At Pueblo Bonito in Chaco Culture National Historical Park, people can hike past the ruins of kivas and great houses.

period, many people began building large pueblos. Archaeologists call these large pueblos great houses.

Pueblo Bonito is the largest pueblo in New Mexico's Chaco Canyon. Portions of the pueblo are five stories tall, and it includes about 800 rooms and 37 kivas. Kivas are round rooms that are built largely underground. People enter by a ladder through the ceiling. Ancient people held religious ceremonies inside kivas.

Archaeologists have discovered trade goods at great houses. The Chimney Rock great house is near

DNA

Puebloan people usually buried their dead outdoors. But in 1896, archaeologists excavated a crypt in Pueblo Bonito. The room contained 14 burials dating from 800 CE to 1130 CE. Connecting rooms contained expensive trade goods, including parrot feathers and turquoise beads. In 2017, scientists took DNA samples from skeletons buried in the crypt. They found that the skeletons had the same mitochondrial DNA. This type of DNA is passed down through women in a family. Some samples were from mothers and daughters, while others were from grandmothers and grandsons. This suggests that authority was passed down through women in a family.

Pagosa Spring in southern Colorado. Archaeologists found pottery there that came from northeastern Arizona. This suggests that ancient people traded inside and outside of the region.

Some Middle Formative people still lived in smaller pueblos. These included up to 20 rooms and were often near farmlands. There was usually a spring nearby for drinking water. Based on these pueblos' location, archaeologists believe good farmland was more important to people than water sources.

MISSISSIPPIAN FARMERS

In eastern North America, the Middle Formative Period spanned from about 800 CE to 1600 CE. It was also called the Mississippian Period. During this time, people grew most of their food, including corn, beans, and squash. They grew gourds and sunflowers too. People also harvested food from rivers and wetlands, gathering fish, shellfish, and waterfowl. They hunted animals such as deer.

The Mississippians lived along rivers that fed into the Mississippi River. People traded along these rivers, traveling in canoes or walking on the prairie grasslands and bluffs. They traded natural resources such as salt, shells, and chert. People also traded pottery and other homemade goods. Mississippian people often traded for copper, which they used to make ceremonial plaques.

Many Mississippians lived within Cahokia and other towns. Others lived in nearby villages. The only remains that archaeologists have found of Mississippian homes are pits, postholes, and wall trenches. Archaeologists look for dark stains in the soil where posts were once sunk into the ground. Homes at the West Lake Quarry site in Missouri were circular and 15 feet (4.6 m) wide. To store food, people at the site made pottery tempered with shells. Tempering is a process that keeps pottery from shattering when it is fired in an oven. People stored pots of food in pits dug into the ground.

PUEBLO III

For the Puebloan peoples, the Late Formative Period was known as Pueblo III. It took place from 1150 CE to 1300 CE. This is when the cliff dwellings that many people think of as pueblos were built. Archaeologists think most cliff dwellings were built after 1225–1230 CE, but it is hard to tell. One way to date a building is to examine its wooden beams. Archaeologists compare

Mesa Verde National Park is home to some of the best-preserved Puebloan cliff dwellings. The largest dwelling at the site is Cliff Palace, which has at least 150 rooms.

tree rings to identify growth patterns such as droughts and rainy periods. One tree ring equals about one year. They use this information to establish dates. But archaeologists think Puebloans reused beams from older buildings. Dates from reused beams reveal when the beams were first cut, not when they were reused.

Pueblo III cliff dwellings were often part of villages. The cliff dwelling would be built at or below a canyon or mesa rim. Other buildings might be built on the slopes near the base of mountains. At Mesa Verde in Colorado,

PUEBLOAN ANCESTORS

In the late 1800s, cliff dwellings in the southwestern United States drew the attention of archaeologists. At this time, they didn't call the people who lived there Puebloan ancestors. They called them the Anasazi. This Navajo term means "ancient enemies." Early archaeologists didn't think their findings had anything to do with modern Puebloan peoples. They researched why the Anasazi had vanished. Today, archaeologists know they did not vanish. Over time, they became today's modern Puebloan peoples. Most modern Ancestral Puebloan people don't like the term Anasazi because of its negative meaning.

some buildings were constructed on top of large boulders.

During Pueblo III, people began using different types of stone tools. At some sites, archaeologists have found metates, or long flat stones used for grinding grains. In Chaco Canyon, archaeologists have also found *tchamahia*. Archaeologists believe these were used as ceremonial hoes.

STRAIGHT TO THE SOURCE

Dr. Paige A. Ford is the station archaeologist at Plum Bayou Mounds in Arkansas. Ford says the mounds tell the story of people who once lived at the site:

> *Mounds are not just constructions that took place all in one go. They contain many features inside of them—fire pits, middens, postholes, and more—that tell us a story of what they were utilized for by people like the Plum Bayou. . . . Plum Bayou Mounds is a ceremonial center, meaning people did not live at this site year-round. Rather, individuals and communities would travel from the surrounding region to this site for rituals, feasts, and other religious and ceremonial events. Each mound at the site has a different story to tell about these activities; each mound contains ritual artifacts, evidence of public structures, and middens, showing us evidence of feasting events, and more.*

Source: Paige A. Ford. "Mound S at Plum Bayou Mounds." *Arkansas Archeological Survey*, Dec. 2022, archeology.uark.edu. Accessed 6 May 2024.

CONSIDER YOUR AUDIENCE

Adapt this passage for a different audience, such as your friends. Write a blog post conveying this information for the new audience. How does your post differ from the original text and why?

CHAPTER THREE

MESOAMERICA

The Olmec people lived in Mesoamerica during the Formative Period. They are the oldest civilization in Mexico. Archaeologists do not know what they called themselves. Olmec was the Aztec name for these people. It means "people of the rubber country," after rubber produced from the *Castilla elastica* tree.

Discoveries of stone carvings led archaeologists to the Olmec. In 1869, José Melgar reported that he had found a

Giant Olmec heads are displayed in museums throughout Mexico. The heads range from about 3.8 feet (1.2 m) to 11 feet (3.4 m) tall.

giant stone head in Veracruz, Mexico. Later, other archaeologists found carved stelae and thrones in the same area.

RUBBER BALLS

The oldest rubber object ever found dates to 1600 BCE. It is a rubber ball found at El Manati, an Olmec site near San Lorenzo. This type of ball was used in a ritual ball game called *tlachtli* or *ollama*. The game is still played in Mexico today. Teams compete on a rectangular court usually measuring up to 65 feet (20 m) long. The rules of the game vary, but players can sometimes score points by hitting the ball through a ring that's attached to the wall surrounding the court. Players often wear protective pads around their waists and hit the ball with their elbows, knees, and hips.

The Olmec built their capital, San Lorenzo, on a river island amid a wetland. Between 1800 BCE and 1400 BCE, they moved 2 million tons (1.8 million metric tons) of earth. This is equal to the weight of 5.5 New York Empire State Buildings. They leveled high spots and filled ravines to create a plateau, or flat hilltop. They built San Lorenzo on the plateau.

Workers lived in wattle-and-daub homes made of wooden stakes and sticks covered in mud or clay. Higher-class people lived in multiroom poured-earth homes. To make these, people poured mud between temporary walls and let it harden. Then they painted the homes.

The Olmec people caught some food, such as fish, turtles, and shrimp, in the wetlands. They also grew maize and may have grown manioc, a root also known as cassava. Archaeologists are still learning more about which foods the Olmec grew and ate.

THE MAYA

In Mesoamerica, the Middle Formative Period ranged from 900 BCE to 300 BCE. People still farmed during this time, and large towns became the center of society. Many towns included political centers where leaders lived. Some towns had religious buildings too. Religious and political leaders were powerful and wealthy, so they could buy things other people could not afford.

A wealthy Olmec leader might own an iron mirror or items made from jade. This is a type of green stone.

As people settled in villages and towns, they developed their own cultures. Different groups came up with their own ways of doing things. They also borrowed ideas from other people.

The Maya were one Middle Formative culture. They are also considered part of the Classic or Post-Classic Period, which came after the Formative. Before they built the large urban centers that many people today think of, the Maya lived in smaller communities. This time in Maya history is considered part of the Formative Period.

The Maya lived in Belize, Guatemala, and Mexico. They settled in the mountains and in lowlands near the ocean. They built cities with large stone temples. Their craftspeople made things out of copper and gold.

One Middle Formative site, Uaxactun, was a Maya religious center. It was abandoned between 900 CE and 1000 CE. Archaeologists discovered the oldest

260-day Maya calendar at Uaxactun. Maya calendars tracked the movements of the sun, moon, and planets. The 260-day calendar was used to schedule religious ceremonies. It includes 260 days, but no months.

Many Maya settlements had observatories, or buildings where priests gathered to observe the movements of the sun and stars. An observatory in a coastal area would be used to locate the rising sun along the horizon. For example, a Maya priest might know that when the sun rose above a certain volcano, it was time for a specific festival.

DISCOVERING UAXACTUN

Uaxactun was discovered in 1916 by Sylvanus Morley. Local guides who helped him reach the ruins called the nearby campsite San Leandro, so that is what Morley first called Uaxactun. Later, the campsite was called Bambonal. Morley decided to give the ruins a name that wouldn't be changed. He called the site Uaxactun, which means "stone 8" in the local Mayan language. The name comes from a calendar date found on a stela at the site.

MAYA CALENDAR
SYMBOLS

The Maya calendar is made up of 260 days. There are 20 different day names, each used 13 times in combination with a number. This graphic shows some of the calendar's symbols. What do you notice about the symbols? How is this calendar similar to or different than modern calendars?

The first day
1 Imix

The 21st day
8 Imix

The second day
2 Ik

The 22nd day
9 Ik

The third day
3 Ak'bal

The 23rd day
10 Ak'bal

The fourth day
4 Kan

The 24th day
11 Kan

Monte Albán was an important Zapotec city located in what is now Oaxaca, Mexico. Today, it is an archaeological site.

Uaxactun was surrounded by a forest, so there were no volcanoes or landmarks in sight. Archaeologists believe this was why the Maya people built tall temples in forested areas. The temples rose above the trees and became landmarks for tracking the rising sun.

ZAPOTEC

In Mesoamerica, the Late Formative Period lasted from about 300 BCE to 250 CE. During this period, regional centers expanded and became political. Strong cities ruled the surrounding countryside and formed city-states. These are cities that govern themselves.

Massive building projects occurred during this time. In Mesoamerica, these buildings were often stone temples, sculptures, and paved stone patios. People may have also built wooden structures, but these structures didn't last because the wood decayed.

The Zapotec writing system is the oldest known form of writing in Mesoamerica, originating as early as 600 BCE. Archaeologists know little about it. The system is based on hieroglyphs, or images. Some of these glyphs depict the heads of people and animals, while others show human feet and hands. There are also glyphs of everyday items such as rattles, arrows, and axes. Archaeologists believe Zapotec hieroglyphs are logographic, meaning each symbol represents a word.

STRAIGHT TO THE SOURCE

Sylvanus Morley discovered Uaxactun with Arthur Carpenter, field director of the Peabody Museum, and a guide named Alfonso. Morley described finding the ruins on May 5, 1916:

> *Between the plain stela and the one Arthur had found was another large stone, prostrate, which had apparently fallen face up and had nothing on it. While I was deciphering the first date, Arthur had . . . found several more stones. Three of these appeared to be altars, and the fourth a broken stela. . . . The altar in front of this stela was 6 feet [1.8 m] in diameter and had nine plain circles on top around the edge. Again, Arthur disappeared and again a shout, this time from both Alfonso and Arthur. They had discovered another stela with glyphs on it. . . . The new find was a large monument with [calendar glyphs] on one side.*

Source: Prudence M. Rice and Christopher Ward, editors. "The Archaeological Field Diaries of Sylvanus Griswold Morley." *Mesoweb*, 2021, mesoweb.com. Accessed 6 May 2024.

BACK IT UP

The author of this passage is using evidence to support a point. Write a paragraph describing the point the author is making. Then write two or three pieces of evidence the author uses to make the point.

CHAPTER FOUR

SOUTH AMERICA

The Early Formative Period in Peru's Andes Mountains is called the Initial Period. It occurred from 1800 BCE to 900 BCE. Most people in the Peruvian coastal region did not initially need to farm to form large settlements. Instead, they harvested birds, shellfish, and fish from the ocean.

One Early Formative and Late Archaic site in Peru is Caral-Supe. It was once a ceremonial center. The people who occupied Caral-Supe from about 1300 BCE to 900 BCE built a

Caral-Supe features the ruins of temples, plazas, and pyramids. The site is considered one of the oldest ancient cities in the Americas.

road and three round, sunken courts. They also built a central plaza and pyramids. Up to 3,000 people lived in Caral-Supe. Most homes were south of the ceremonial area. All buildings were constructed of stone blocks joined with mud. People also lived on farms around Caral-Supe. They grew squash, beans, and potatoes.

FOOD REMAINS

Alto Salaverry, dating from 2500 BCE to 1800 BCE, is a site on the Peruvian coast. Archaeologists have found ancient food remains there. These include sharks, fish called bonitos, and shellfish called mussels. In several communities, archaeologists examined human skeletons. They found a pattern of bone growth in the skeletons' inner ears. People develop this pattern when they dive repeatedly in cold water. Because of this, archaeologists can tell that ancient people dove to catch sharks, bonitos, and mussels.

ANDEAN EARLY INTERMEDIATE PERIOD

For Andean cultures, the Late Formative Period is known as the Early Intermediate Period. It occurred from around 200 BCE to 600 CE. During this time, some Andean cultures had chiefdoms, in which one person ruled over several settlements. The chief and his family outranked others. Lower-class people had less wealth and power.

During the Late Formative, the Andean population grew from several hundred thousand people to four or five million. One culture, the Moche, had a population of about 25,000 people. Their territory stretched 215 miles (346 km) along the Peruvian coast.

The Moche people developed an

ANCIENT TEETH

Archaeologists have learned about what Moche people ate by examining their teeth. Archaeologists examined plaque on the teeth of 12 Moche skeletons. Plaque forms from tiny particles of food and saliva between people's teeth. These particles were preserved on the skeletons' teeth. In the plaque, archaeologists found amaranth and red algae from deep ocean water. They also found green algae from fresh water and bits of sea sponges. Based on these findings, they think Moche people ate fish, mollusks, and seaweed from the Moche River.

FORMATIVE PERIOD STAGES

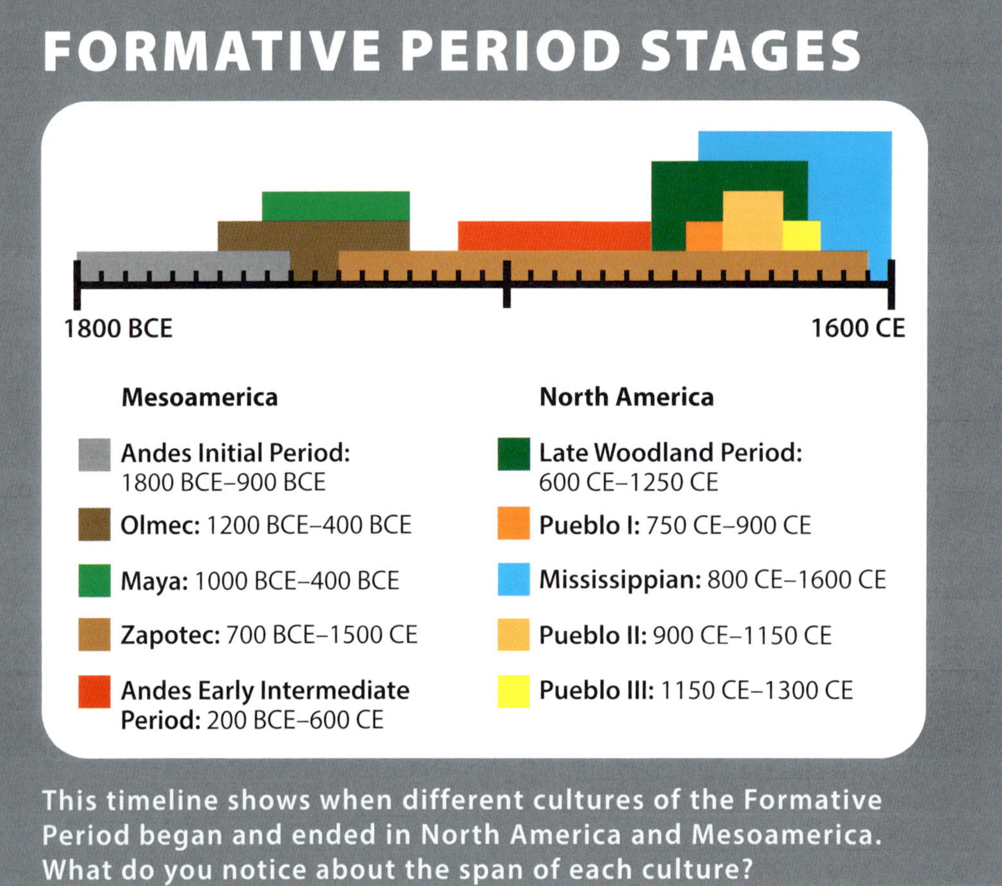

This timeline shows when different cultures of the Formative Period began and ended in North America and Mesoamerica. What do you notice about the span of each culture?

advanced irrigation system, which helped them grow food. This allowed the population to flourish. Their irrigation system involved mud canals that extended down mountainsides into the valleys. Because the canals were built of mud, they had to be carefully designed. If water flowed too slowly, the canals would silt up as particles of soil settled out of the water. If water ran too quickly, it wore down the canals. Large groups of workers cleaned the canals each year.

During the Formative Period, many cultures developed across the Americas. These cultures often went through similar stages but grew at different paces. Although Formative peoples traded goods and ideas, their cultures differed. Peruvian cultures relied on seafood and crops, while Mississippians journeyed in canoes. Archaeological sites built by these Formative cultures can still be visited today. The period set the stage for future periods of history.

FURTHER EVIDENCE

Chapter Four includes information about Formative civilizations in South America, such as the Moche. What is the main point of this chapter? What key evidence supports this point? Go to the article about Andean civilizations at the website below. Find a quote from the website that supports the chapter's main point.

ANDEAN CIVILIZATIONS

abdocorelibrary.com/formative-period

IMPORTANT DATES

1800–1400 BCE
The Olmec create a flattened hilltop on an island. They build their capital, San Lorenzo, at this site.

1500 BCE
The Early Formative Period begins in Mesoamerica.

1300–900 BCE
The Peruvian ceremonial site of Caral-Supe is in use. It is the site of a plaza with a temple and round courts.

100 BCE–100 CE
People build two burial mounds at Crowley's Ridge, Arkansas. The mounds contain valuable trade goods.

750 CE
The Pueblo I period begins in the southwestern United States.

900–1000
Uaxactun, a Maya religious center, is abandoned.

1100
The Mississippian settlement of Cahokia thrives. About 15,000 to 20,000 people live at the site.

1869
José Melgar discovers an Olmec stone head in Veracruz, Mexico.

1916
Sylvanus Morley discovers Uaxactun, a Maya religious center in Guatemala.

2018
Archaeologists discover evidence about the people who once lived at Cahokia.

STOP AND THINK

Tell the Tale

Chapter One of this book discusses what visitors can see at Cahokia Mounds. Imagine you are visiting this historical site. Write 200 words about the mounds and their surroundings. What do you notice about the site?

Surprise Me

Chapter Three discusses different Formative cultures in Mesoamerica. After reading this book, what two or three facts about Mesoamerican Formative cultures were most surprising? Write a few sentences about each fact. Why did you find each fact surprising?

You Are There

This book discusses Puebloan dwellings in the southwestern United States. Imagine you are traveling back in time to a Puebloan settlement. Write a letter home telling your friends about what it is like to live in a Puebloan dwelling. Be sure to add plenty of detail to your notes.

Why Do I Care?

The Formative Period happened a very long time ago. But that doesn't mean you can't think about how the period affected modern life. What tools and inventions did Formative cultures use that people still use today?

GLOSSARY

archaeologist
a person who studies human history through artifacts and other remains

ceremonial
of or relating to religious rites and celebrations

civilization
an advanced stage of social development

crypt
a room used for a burial

drought
a period of little to no rainfall

excavate
to dig up the ground to uncover artifacts or remains

glyph
a symbol or picture used to represent a word or sound

irrigation
the practice of bringing water to land for farming

mesa
an isolated, flat-topped hill with steep sides

prehistoric
taking place before written records

ritual
of or relating to a ceremony that is always performed the same way

stela
an upright stone slab

ONLINE RESOURCES

To learn more about the Formative Period, visit our free resource websites below.

Visit **abdocorelibrary.com** or scan this QR code for free Common Core resources for teachers and students, including vetted activities, multimedia, and booklinks, for deeper subject comprehension.

Visit **abdobooklinks.com** or scan this QR code for free additional online weblinks for further learning. These links are routinely monitored and updated to provide the most current information available.

LEARN MORE

Howell, Izzi. *The Genius of the Maya*. Crabtree, 2020.

Hudak, Heather C. *The Archaic Period*. Abdo, 2025.

Milosavljevich, Stefan. *Tales of Ancient Worlds*. Neon Squid, 2022.

INDEX

About the Author

Sue Bradford Edwards is a nonfiction author. She writes for children and teens, working from her home in Saint Louis, Missouri. She studied archaeology and history in college and worked as an archaeological illustrator, drawing funeral medallions buried in a historic cemetery in Saint Louis. Her books for young readers include *The Ancient Maya*, *Russia*, *Australia*, and *Cave and Mine Survival Stories*.